REVERSA

C000271317

Kate Rhodes

Reversal

ENITHARMON PRESS

First published in 2005
by the Enitharmon Press
26B Caversham Road
London NW5 2DU

www.enitharmon.co.uk

Distributed in the UK by
Central Books
99 Wallis Road
London E9 5LN

Distributed in the USA and Canada
by Dufour Editions Inc.
PO Box 7, Chester Springs
PA 19425, USA

© Kate Rhodes 2005

ISBN 1 904634 07 9

Enitharmon Press gratefully acknowledges
the financial support of Arts Council
England, London.

British Library Cataloguing-in-Publication Data.
A catalogue record for this book is available
from the British Library.

Volume 1 in the Enitharmon New Poets Series,
dedicated to the memory of Alan Clodd (1918–2002)
and generously funded by his estate.

Typeset in Bembo by Servis Filmsetting Ltd
and printed in England by
Antony Rowe Ltd

For Dave Pescod

ACKNOWLEDGEMENTS

Poems in this collection have appeared in: *Borderlines, The Interpreter's House, Iota, Magma, The New Writer, The North, Orbis, Other Poetry, Poetry Monthly, Poetry Review, Reactions 3, Seam, Smiths Knoll, Spiked, Staple, The Yellow Crane.*

I would like to thank Sarah Shaw, Helen Johnson, Jessica Penrose, Elizabeth Foy, Sally Cline and the Cambridge Women Writers Group, Carole Bromley, Mike Barlow, Joyce Lambert, Liz Cashdan, Rob Locke and Pauline Rowe.

Many thanks to the Hawthornden Literary Institute for granting me a fellowship during 2004.

CONTENTS

Measuring America

Familial

Paradise Road

MEASURING AMERICA

OUT OF WATER

In a fug of heat and argument
the map evaporates, abandons us here
tasting iced tea gingerly
for the first time.

Inside the air's so cold
my spine freezes to the metal chair.
Not far away a man fishes,
shirtless and glimmering.

He spreads his small net
as a waiter casts his cloth
deftly, with one smart flick.
It comes back shaking with life,

silver beads in a fancy choker.
He throws a fish into a bucket,
its whole body a wagging protest.
One by one the others follow

until the bucket's full.
Stronger than the rest
just one fish leaps clear,
fails to find the stream.

When the map's rehydrated
we'll get back into the car,
try not to squirm in our seats
or bicker, or be too English.

EMPIRE STATE SKY-DIVING

Forty-eight, forty-nine, fifty,
the storeys went by like years.

With every floor
the elevator boy yawned through

you grew wiser to the fact
there was no coming back.

Forget the Chrysler and the World Bank,
it had to be this for your diving board

for its glassy look,
the way it poked its finger at the stars.

It took nine seconds to somersault
onto the cover of *Time Life,*

long enough to see yourself kicking at gravity,
each breath framed in black and white.

Clasping the breeze,
the city above you, now below you

the street held out its cradle,
empty and rocking.

I see you arrive at last
open-mouthed

eyes snagged on the skyline.
You dropped from the monster's hands.

This road's finer than a bikini strap
but it's not how it seemed on *MGM,*
Bogart lied about *Key Largo.*

There's nothing to pause for –
not love, not treasure – just a shell midden,
crumbling and never visited.

It takes nine hours to reach
the end of America's rope,
to find the air kissing my neck

Caribbean and softer than breath.
The men here are so young,
smiling, hand in hand.

You wouldn't think Hurricane Mitch
danced through here last month
tipping cabins from their pastel stilts.

The harbour tore so cleanly in two
I can trace the straight rend
from Mallory to the cemetery.

The graves pile up here
one sarcophagus pushing another down,
ten or twelve lives

stacked up, facing Cuba.
It's so near they must feel it
in the balls of their feet,

the marimba,
that easy syncopation,
a million miles from jive.

NEW YORK, NEW YORK

The elevator man used to give me
lessons in jazz. It was like poetry, he said,
unpredictable, heavenly.
His days ticked past, heavy with messages
from sidewalk to sky.

Up there on the ninetieth floor
even the skyline had a jazz logic –
those buildings used to dance in the heat,
tall, thin women shimmying
to the traffic's noise.

Black and yellow cubes of sound
parcelled at their feet in Mondrian squares,
till sound abandoned them.
Why pretend you can make
an accommodation to the silence

you find, when the birds
have given up the sky?
Start spreading the news –
the Chrysler has grown suddenly taller,
raised its one sharp fist to the sky.

UTOPIA PARKWAY

(for Joseph Cornell)

Nails line up on the shelf.
He knows he must strike
each one, steadily
until his dreams are fixed.

Oceans and continents
line the basement walls,
birds hide in the darkness
flightless, afraid to sing.

If you're prepared to squint
drop a coin in the slot,
there's a peephole to the galaxies.
Black and white, shining

constellations stolen
from last month's *Science*
unfold in glossy light years.
Tonight on Utopia Parkway

world after world
is wrapped and stored,
each one hermetic,
ready for use.

TO DAMIEN HIRST'S SHARK

Unrepentant, honest,
with its Peter Benchley sneer,
your face is always
a killer's face.

Your eyes snap shut on me
pin-hole small,
obscenely focused.
No wonder they model cars on you,

your striated gills are sleek by design.
From this distance you could strike me,
a muscled fist
in a tight leather glove.

When I lived in Winter Park
you were still alive.
The radio spat out the truth about you,
that boy on Vero Beach was eight, maybe nine,

they found his torn shoulders
on Merritt Island,
then a few days later,
his head.

After that, for months
you inspected me coolly
through the shark cage
of my nightmares.

Smiling your fixed grin
you always found me,
your keen fins cut
the pattern of my fears.

You prove we can't sell
our ogres to Saatchi and Saatchi,
they still catch us in the shallows
at night, by stealth.

SUN IN AN EMPTY ROOM

Edward Hopper, 1962

I would say still, not empty.
The kind of hard American stillness
you come across in hotel lobbies,
in the hour between the porter's last drink
and the kitchen opening at dawn.

Sunlight arrived by 4 a.m., strong enough
to brand its initials on the drab wall –
two hard-edged columns, tall as doorways.
As if you could step straight through
into glory or the heart of summer.

Leaves rail against the locked window
but nature has been evicted.
Light is the sole occupant.
It plans to live here like Greta Garbo,
unphotographed and alone.

LOOKING FOR TENNESSEE

On the freeway every other car
travels more purposefully.
They have the right to over-take,
roof-racks loaded with reality
beginning legitimate breaks.

In Miami the buildings sneer.
Even the Everglades disapprove,
on the guided tour, pelicans hiss.
By Key Largo the sky glares,
it's a fixed, dismissive blue.

Your house hides behind jacarandas,
no one answers the bell.
Everyone I see is looking for you.
At the waterfront Stanley's alone
drinking beer and bourbon chasers.

I can see why.
Blanche is dancing on the sidewalk
to music only she can hear.
In the morning she'll follow me
back to Acacia Avenue.

If I need to I'll smash a window.
Anything to catch sight of you
white-suited at your desk,
dreaming of Taormina
while Merlo cleans the pool.

TARPON SPRINGS

Hands tight on the steering wheel,
half a state's lost in an undertow
of diners and shopping marts.
At last the car stops here,
but it's too late to see the river
this town's christened for.

In the motel it's hard to sleep.
Headlights swim in a circuit,
race past pictures and stains.
The guidebook tells me
ten Greek families settled here,
made a living diving for sponges.

I turn out the lights, try not to see
those boys, choking in black water
for three minutes at a time,
until they rise, gasping into the sun
like line-caught fish –
too often with empty hands.

AUSTIN, TEXAS

Sweating in Mexico's reflected heat
houses rest on *Blue Velvet* lawns,
confederate butterflies
dancing above every porch.

It's a long walk back
through the sticky Republican air.
All the bars sealed, bottles of tequila
painted onto mirrored windows.

I keep walking but my shadow dips inside
to see the gauchos dreaming
over *Cerveza Gold*,
waitresses paying out shots.

The street names are a shopping list
of Mexican promises:
Piedras Negras, San Cristobal,
Sierra Madres.

From here it's just a three-day drive
to air you don't have to filter,
temples that map the constellations –
mine after mine of fools' gold.

CELEBRATION

The streets here are perfectly drawn,
houses selected from the Disney catalogue
pre-fabricated in make-believe and money.

Town planners keep the lawns in order.
Birds and shadows have been erased,
even the seasons have been edited.

This year there will be no Fall.
It's expensive, wind machines on the sidewalks
billowing storms of red paper leaves.

But Christmas is still compulsory.
Residents carry lanterns for the tourists,
sleigh bells rattle all day through open windows.

Tonight the artificial snow drifts will be rebuilt,
every footstep removed, so that tomorrow
Celebration will look just as it did today.

A PIECE OF AMERICAN SKY

I found it in the remnant shop
cloudless, not more than a metre wide.
At first it was postcard bright,
the glitter in a Miami pool,
then pale as celluloid, a backdrop
for cowboys to ride through.

In my hand it felt insubstantial
glossed with rain, hissing with sounds
stolen from the Everglades –
pelicans, snake birds, distant planes.
Back home it abandoned its folds,
rose shimmering to the ceiling.

All afternoon the sunshine warmed my face
then I had to leave the room.
I didn't want to see it blackened
pierced through with stars,
or worse, snagged on a floorboard,
brightness clouded with dust.

TAKE JOURNEYS IN YOUR MIND

Henry David Thoreau

Keen to follow your advice
I've packed my suitcase
put on sun cream, closed my eyes.

The departure's perfect.
In a new convertible, roof down
a young man waits for me.

The sun's too bright
but he could almost be Elvis
fresh-faced, half my age.

We cross the Atlantic at ninety –
a smooth blue highway
only we can ride.

But already he's homesick.
He jumps out in Memphis,
kisses me goodbye.

The road is Hollywood familiar,
it could be Sunset Strip
until it peters into sand,

leaves me stranded in the desert
gas tank empty, without a phone.
Now I'll have to hitch a ride

back to where I left myself
propped up in bed,
passport in my hand.

CROUPIER

My boss says *don't pity them*
but when my shift's done
they trail me,
pockets jangling
with left-over hopes.

By now the sky's let go of black,
edged into blue.
The sidewalk shuffles
answers and questions.
My father's asking

who taught you those tricks?
He didn't want me
to be like him,
tired, white collar grey
from the city's disease.

But I'm still here at the table
fingers so slick
you hardly see them,
paying my chances
into other people's hands.

MEASURING AMERICA

It was Jefferson's idea,
drop a grid over the new world
slice it into wedding cake squares.

Armed with geometry
the surveyors headed west,
laid down their chains.

Not just New York
but Wisconsin, the Dakotas,
Medicine Bow Mountains,

the Grand Canyon sectioned,
until even the rain fell
in spans and cubits.

Bethany, Alma and Beatrice –
realtors piled cities into boxes
christened for their wives.

By California they ran out of rope,
sat under palm trees
dividing the ocean with their eyes.

FAMILIAL

REVERSAL

I can see now it was a mistake
to back my car out of the drive.
Since then the road looks historic
and the future's in the mirror, blurred.

I'm tempted to pull over
but the hard shoulder's bumper to bumper,
full of memories, badly parked.
Miles back I saw a man I used to know.

At least this time
I know well enough not to stop.
With each junction towns grow paler,
hotels in candy pink, baby blue.

By the time I reach your house
you'll be straight-backed,
talking clearly, in the lawn print dress
you always wore.

We'll sit in the garden for hours,
watch the shadows shorten.
Tomorrow you'll be alone
on the swings sailing backwards,

or reading stories from right to left.
You won't have to miss me,
by the time morning comes
I won't even be imaginary.

MY FATHER WORE ETERNAL CLOTHES

Opposite me on the tube
my father's ghost looks tired.
He's been shopping, posthumously
the bags at his feet not quite real.

He's hard to see, but I can tell
his soul's wrapped still
in the worsted coat
he said would last forever.

He seems relieved,
freed at last from the urn
my mother dusts every day.
On the brass plaque

he's named and dated,
catalogued – as if she knows
she might forget.
He's determined not to see me.

Nothing I have on will last,
cheap boots, a worn-out scarf.
He's gone before the next stop,
clothes folded on his seat.

Corduroys in plush furrows,
Pink's shirt hard with starch
and on my lap, toes shining
his resurrected brogues.

THREE PHOTOS OF MY FATHER IN
REVERSE ORDER

This is how you liked us
symmetrical,
in an orderly row,
a Sunday-best child on either knee.
Your wife's skirt balloons
with Fifties prosperity.
You're in the middle,
not quite smiling.

The wireless is dying
without its Bakelite shell,
metal guts spill across the table.
It's at your mercy.
Invalided out after a month,
too many war time broadcasts
have taught you a new smile, humourless
as if you've had the final say.

Is this Southend or Brighton?
On the black and white pier
you're no more than a schoolboy
and that girl is nobody's wife.
Her hair sections pieces of sun
in Thirties geometric lines.
I never saw that smile you're wearing,
not in my lifetime.

FEATHERS

The clerk searches, but can't find him.
If he'd seen active service
he'd be safe in her computer
numbered, against medals and wounds.

He used to roll up his sleeve –
on his forearm two scars, shiny as coins.
From a bullet he said,
in this side, out the other.

He must have borrowed
his night-time raids from the wireless,
artillery rattling at second hand.
A whole war pinched from bulletins.

Maybe he ducked
through five years in an office
pretending to be frail?
I don't blame him.

I'd do the same.
But I want to know how it felt
to spend a lifetime
waiting to be caught,

dreaming of feathers
bright clouds of them,
floating through the letterbox
or pinned to his door.

THE DOORSTEP

I try not to go back
but I'm driven there at night,
in the old Morris
smelling of leather and fear.

My father hides under the lime tree,
yellow handkerchief leaves
wrap him in sticky cover.
He's left me on the doorstep.

Marble, grey and veined,
they paid me to wipe its dirty face.
I can see inside the lion's mouth,
its copper roar *Brasso* clean.

My father has disappeared,
the car too is dissolving.
There are no footsteps.
No one will come.

SALVATION

Every Sunday the hymns
carry the same guarantee –
never too late to be a better man.
Home by noon
for a drop of the hard stuff,
for the hard change from quiet man
to bully, loud-breathed
enraged by tiny sounds.

He must wonder
why rooms grow silent before him
like a welcome in reverse.
At nine o'clock it's safe
to come back downstairs.
By now he's bent-kneed, staggering,
his wife's free
to make her approach.

Mouth drawn in a tight line,
her words are stoppered.
She knows she'll have to carry him
up two long flights,
another weekend over.
On Monday's clean slate
he'll write his motto –
never too late to be a better man.

FINGERS

I've lost most of you now.
Your post-war suits have faded,
birthday surprises broken or given away.

But I can't forget how you could
make your hand a tall man strolling;
fingernail feet kicking at daisies.

He could vault over jam jars,
almost drown in the sugar bowl,
always come through.

He'd free fall to the valley
of my wrist without a harness –
just for the breeze in his hair.

At night the ghosts of your fingers
index and middle,
still come looking for me

suddenly cautious
afraid of drowning, in the frozen sea
of my white sheets.

FAMILIAL

My grandmother's waiting upstairs.
When she wants tea,
the lavatory, someone to moan to,
she beats the ceiling with her stick.

My father keeps out of the way,
spends hours fiddling with the car.
Right now he's in the garage
hiding wine bottles by the door.

My mother's at evening prayers,
on her knees, hands clasped
pleading with God to guard my sister
in case she's led astray.

Too late. She's on the phone
whispering about sex.
*Come round at nine
my parents are going out.*

Face down on my bed
I'm wallowing in comics.
Spiderman's ready for a rescue –
any second now, he'll land.

DOT

In my picture your mouth is pursed
into a photographer's smile.
Your grey hair hides under your one smart hat.

You saved for it, week on week,
the black cloche buried in cellophane
between funeral and funeral.

I see you
at the Butler sink,
hands scrubbed to a raw mottle,

commanding a meal into being,
slicing, scraping, whipping
the food onto our plates.

Around you
the dog knew not to be canine,
giddiness would not be tolerated.

The shepherdesses
caught in pink china stays
never broke rank on your mantelpiece.

The last of thirteen
your name always bottomed the list,
your dresses came from the scraps

and leavings of your sisters' worn out nighties.
No wonder your voice was sharp enough
to slice a crowd.

You weathered to a greying whetstone,
rinsed and well-used
but always definite.

You were the last out of the door.
Your family's perfect copperplate
full-stop.

MY GRANDPARENTS MET IN 1922

At the end of the line for lemonade
he found her
at the Methodist dance.
He recognised her patience,
her threadbare dress,
the Marcel wave she fixed herself,
her scent of coal tar soap and home.

Last in an inventory of brothers
he could see she was the same –
the final child, unexpected
smaller than the rest.
When the Last Waltz played
they clung together, eked out the steps
cautiously, afraid of waste.

CUTLERY

Not keen to be saved
it's hidden itself in the loft
between dressing-up boxes, mirrors,
stacks of uncomfortable chairs.

On the kitchen table
the canteen opens easily –
tarnished families of spoons,
forks clenched in velvet hollows.

Solid silver. A gift from her mother.
The box shifts slowly
from her hands to mine,
heavy as a child.

She looks relieved.
On the car seat next to me
it whispers, secrets rattling
between handles and tines.

THE MOVING VAN

Now that we're done it's clear
your wing-backed chair, the table, beds,
have left no room for the past.

All our months together,
a drift of spent postage stamps
I'll paste here, inside this album.

My father's sadness, my mother's praise
should stay together. I'll wrap them
with these bookends, carefully, in gauze.

The smile the sun coaxed
out of you at Cedar Key
will be safe in the blanket box.

That leaves just old friendships
and first love to wad in cotton wool.
I'll keep them by me. You can drive.

TALKING TO GIANTS

My friend's son has come to stay,
his parents are separating
but they keep telling him
nothing has to change.

At breakfast he keeps his eyes
fixed on the table,
manages two spoonfuls
forgets to chew.

He tells me about his dream.
Giants come looking for him,
standing by the front door
his eyes are level with their ankles.

He uses a loudhailer, begs them to go
but they wait in the street,
tripping over cars
knocking down lampposts.

Later, on my way to the shops
all I can see is damage.
The tarmac's cratered,
houses have been demolished.

I should have drawn the curtains.
They might see him,
matchstick thin on the sofa
hiding by the TV.

CHARITY

My sister's on the phone
giving me the benefit of her advice.
I should go out more,
worry less, get myself a man.

Starting with lunch
I need lessons in pleasure –
flirting with waiters, liqueurs,
triple chocolate mousse.

She knows I'm broke
I hate dresses that cling,
but we have to go shopping
look for something sexy, in red.

I don't know why I'm smiling
when she says, tonight it's glad-rags,
taxis there and back
vodka in a hip-flask in her bag.

I can see her now, sequinned
giving away dances,
handing out drinks,
never charging anyone, anything.

THE ORCHARD

Roots slide behind skirtings,
twigs tap the emulsion sky.
It's expensive, his savings vanish
in a spectrum of green.

He's growing it for his wife.
Thick branches to silence
the neighbours' whispers:
she won't be coming home.

At night he paints apples,
golden and coarse-skinned.
Home by October,
she inspects the damage

woodpeckers have done to the wall,
windfalls rotting on the floor.
She tells him *it's lovely,*
and in a way it is.

Lovely that he's kept busy
after all her nights awake
on the ward, fretting
about how he'd cope alone.

MEMORY CARDS

Bumpy with *Copydex* and hope
I found them in your bureau,
the pack you made
to help me read.

Words cut from magazines
with pictures to match –
grainy mountains,
moons you drew yourself.

We played with them
until letters chased
across the page, flat-out
in sentence-long races.

When I visited you today
I brought photos –
York Minster, Dad at fifty
in his best suit.

You couldn't put a name
to your sister's face,
or the village in the Dales
where you grew up.

We should have planned for this,
written an inventory
stored words in boxes,
anchored them with weights.

DIVINING

My mother's been crying all day.
Naked on the settee, unthinkably small
her face and throat are cloaked in wrinkles.
She can't be consoled.

I have to find the source of her tears.
Is it in her wardrobe?
Some expensive item
that failed to make her new?

In the study I'm getting warmer.
Her father's bureau perhaps?
Dark, coffin wood
too heavy ever to leave the house.

Maybe it's the trinkets
ganging up on the mantelpiece?
Dresden cows grazing on dust,
the silver lion menacing her.

In the bathroom I discover it at last,
a steady trickle – the tub's almost full.
Who will sing to her,
blow bubbles, pretend to splash?

The only child but not a child,
I guide her to the water
cradle her,
lift her in.

THE TABLE

I knew you'd died when the table arrived.
Packed in tatty cardboard
the legs came first, then a few days later
the body, the tusks, the trunk.

The eyes were separate.
Wrapped in surgical cotton wool
they looked up at me, too moist,
too knowing, to handle without gloves.

I had to piece it all together.
The legs walked into accommodating sockets,
but the tusks bit me,
fighting into place.

You must have thought of me,
trapped between the petals and thorns
of the wallpaper roses in your room.
You must have longed for mysterious presents.

Your elephant fills my study,
it smells of teak oil and the Nineteenth Century.
His toenails are chips of ivory.
In the dark they shine, like perfect teeth.

INVENTORY

Six marble eggs,
each one holding tight
the memory of heat.

Three photos of the Black Sea
without a wave or a breeze,
images to sleep by.

One blanket I gave you
folded and coarse with sand,
the grained history of picnics.

I thought there was nothing left to count.
No more objects
sticky with memories and time

until I saw your shoes
huddled by the skirting, worn beyond use,
hiding from me in pairs.

THE HANOI LADY FISH

Too old to work
she can still see the factory,
great ribs shining
beached on the horizon.

She traded her years there
painting fishes,
hands scarred from solder
and chasing metal fins.

Today her daughter
has brought her a new fish,
red and gilt,
bigger than her fist.

It inspects her
with a carp's mean stare.
Her daughter shows her
how to open its jaw.

Tiny, painted with the waves
they must learn to ride,
on an umbilical
of fisherman's twine,

the Hanoi lady fish gasps out
child after surprising child.

CHILDERMAS

The opposite of Christmas
the room's still full of candles,
a crowd of flames
waving, not quite grown.

If I close my eyes
I can see them in their gangs
wearing the uniform of summer.
Arms and legs bare

in the middle of some game
that couldn't wait;
chained together like daisies
brother, sister, brother.

By the river
they learned to strip willow,
plait bangles, green and shining
for their mothers' worn-out arms.

On that day the reeds
too busy whispering,
obeying the wind,
were not good mothers.

Imagine a thousand children
sleeping on a riverbank.
Then look again, imagine them
never waking.

I can't picture it
but I can count the flames,
bright, always moving,
nowhere near burnt down.

PARADISE ROAD

ALFRED WALLIS AT ST IVES

The fishermen head north
into blacker and blacker sea,
riding the boats that drift past
at night, when you close your eyes.

You don't have to look to see them,
the wooden trawlers of your childhood,
each net and window, each funnel and sail
scratched out in blue and red.

You know it's a wonder you've found a house here
built like the maritime years – boards on a kilter.
You sway from room to room
with a sailor's rolling gait.

In this place you know how it feels
to be selected from the beach,
pocketed for a moment or two
in a place of safety.

But the voices at high tide
are a singing interference,
telling you every stone
on the beach is your equal.

The sea's calling you strange names today
or maybe it's only the gulls bawling.
Either way there'll be no rest
until you've caught those waves

as you see them.
Green and silver, the ragged claws
of the monsters they've drowned,
copied straight from a child's worst dreams.

THE WELCOME

It's me, I'm home,
I greet the house every day at six.

It doesn't always care,
front door narrow as a grudging smile.

It keeps warmth and sunlight to itself,
absorbed in its pale walls.

But some days when I take off my coat,
drop my briefcase in the hall,

the bedrooms tumble
down the stairs to greet me,

and the hat stand
(which has been aloof for days)

stretches out its arms.

NOT TODAY, THANK YOU

I watch you struggle with the gate,
your smart blue suit a carbon copy
of the smart blue suit
my husband used to wear.

But whatever you're selling
insurance, double glazing, God,
I'm not buying. My cupboard's full –
dusters folded in yellow families.

You don't need to give me a brochure,
the windows are staying.
They've kept watch on the street
unblinking for a hundred years.

And if it's Jehovah you're pedalling
there's no need. He talks to me all day.
Only at night he's silent, asleep
between the pages of my *King James*.

MR HARRIS RETIRES NEXT YEAR

From the top deck of the bus
childhood landmarks
quiver behind billboards,
shops with assumed names.

She's going back
to the teacher who bullied her,
determined to have her say,
make him feel ashamed.

She has her questions planned.
What made you do it?
How did you choose
which children to ridicule?

Grey-haired in his tight suit,
teeth still either perfect or false,
he meets her in the staff room
tells her he doesn't have long.

But he's pleased to see her.
It means so much when pupils
come back, to thank me
for everything I've done.

BIRDS OF PARADISE

Honestly, they came to me,
girl after girl.

They had reason to be thankful
for my hospitality,

they would have lasted a week
maybe two, without their little rooms.

And you can see
it's a clean establishment.

Even at my age
there are flowers in the hall.

Of course I saw them going out,
flamingo pink shoes, scorching red dresses.

I was the same. Dancing on a Saturday,
sequins and feathers. Here's a photo, look.

So when they told me
they liked a good time, I understood.

I saw him go in, the one from the TV,
on every day with his wife.

I just thought they had
friends in high places.

I'm seventy-nine, you know.
I had no idea, honestly.

RENDEZVOUS

Rain strafes the roof of my car.
Nothing here but the sea

two shops – closed,
a straggle of bungalows.

A sign on the hotel door
promises to be *back by six*.

Understanding blinks on
with headlight certainty.

His clever, stockbroker wife
wouldn't be seen dead here

or worse still, alive. Of course,
that's why he picked it.

Too tired to drive home
I'll wait for him in the car,

run down my batteries
tuning-in to the news.

GURDWARA WEDDING

You asked me to come
but your mother's waiting
on the steps of the temple
smiling, welcoming guests.

Before I've climbed the steps
her arms are folded.
Your brother looks away
not sure who's wrong or right.

Either way, she won't let me in
says it's best if I don't wait.
Through the doors I hear sitars
a drum, something like a flute.

I can picture your bride
face hidden, hands brittle
with the outlines of flowers.
On the other side of the door

she holds the hem of your coat.
Before I get back to the car
her wrist will be tied to yours
with a chunni of yellow silk.

DINNER WITH SANJAY

When your wife comes
she'll bring India with her,
as much of it as she can carry
in a holdall and two suitcases –

ganthias, the sari she married in,
hand-printed in red and gold.
You're telling me this while you
chop coriander, serve the dhal.

Dishes crowd the table.
You're telling me
you had no choice,
you had to leave her there.

Too ill to travel,
she needed her sisters by her
to watch and listen while she sleeps.
We've hardly begun

but already you're asking me,
why is it in this country
when you fall sick
your family forget you, walk away?

I can see my mother
confused, a danger to herself,
tin foil lunches brought to her
each day by different strangers.

Rice mounds up on my plate.
When my wife comes you will be friends,
she'll cook for you.
It will be better than this.

CRAZY GOLF

We've left your family playing
by the Egyptian towers,
the tiny stucco cliffs.

Walking the tide line
I'm having trouble
seeing you as you are now,

grey-haired, thirty-nine,
beginning to be worn.
I've tried rubbing my eyes

but your skin, your mouth
keep slipping back to how they were
before womanhood bit,

when you had pockets
full of phone numbers,
and all men were fools.

You're telling me something
but the sea keeps tuning you out.
It's oil slick brown today,

rising like panic.
You're telling me
about the sex you've been having

with some man, not your husband.
It's nothing much
it won't change anything

but you need it,
it fuels you,
you're sexy again.

Somehow we've come full circle,
we're back at the *Crazy Golf.*
Your daughters are excited.

They fall on you
waving their scorecards.
The game's over.

BLUEBELLS

Men stopped giving her flowers.
In her garden, frosted and dried,
the winter plants were a lifetime's
spent bouquets.

She needed to give herself a present.
A bathroom with no mirrors,
white towels to wallow in,
a tub deep enough for remembering.

She had to find the perfect blue,
not iris, not midnight,
the sky's watchfulness
two minutes before dark.

In the paint shop
the young man listened carefully –
mixed lilac, cobalt, amethyst,
a practised conjuror.

They saw it spin into colour,
or he did, she watched
the blackness of his hair.
No grey, he must be half her age.

His eyes when he noticed her
were a quick green sea change.
I can tell he said, when you dream,
you dream of bluebells.

BOOTS

I can picture what you need
size ten, the perfect pair.
The pair to make you relax,
put your feet up, stay.

Brown Oxford brogues
a W of leather to warm your heel,
toe-caps hand-stitched,
needled through with holes.

Or Chelsea boots,
tight at the ankle
to remind you of your youth.
There's no reason to stop

beside this shop window,
but I stand here looking
for more than a minute,
face close to the glass.

They are thigh-length
dangerous five inch spikes,
leather gloves for my thighs
close-fitting as a stocking.

Just for a second
I see myself pulling them on,
marching, without falling
right to the front of the queue.

CIRCULAR BREATHING

Music sifted through every wall
Art Blakey on the radio,
your clarinet dropping notes on the steps.

In August the others went home.
We took the record player out into the yard,
drank beer, flirted, learned how to jive.

At The Vortex the saxophonist
babbled octaves without surfacing,
phrases mixing like a madman's thoughts.

You told me about circular breathing.
One finger on my breastbone you said
take a breath, keep it shallow, here.

The room went round. You told me
I could show you, or we could go to bed.
I wish now I'd shown more self-control.

You could have taught me
to breathe anti-clockwise, inhale summers,
back to the kitchen's cracked tiles,
A Love Supreme wafting through the door.

CASABLANCA

Every day repeats in soft focus
under make-up and cut-lights,
no rest between takes.

Polishing glasses, pouring shots,
I've got the measure at last
of a margarita and a whiskey sour.

The piano always falters on F$^\sharp$,
while the room registers
the symmetry of Ilsa's face.

I'll have to wait ten scenes
before she gets her passport and leaves.
Then Sam will play his songs for me

and Rick will sit up, pay attention
when I sashay towards him
in my red silk dress.

ONE NIGHT WITH DAVID BECKHAM

For the time being it's feasible
that he's here with me
in a de luxe hotel,
combat trousers
falling from his hips.

We can see the river,
Hammersmith and Chiswick
float by on a slow conveyor.
I notice blue plaques on houses
his golden skin.

Then he breaks the news –
he's short of cash.
He wants me to pay the bill.
The phone rings. His agent's warning
this is a nightmare, I'm not his wife.

When I wake up
I try to scramble back into the dream
as if it was waiting,
engines running
like a stretch limousine.

JAGUAR XKR

Sleek, affluent black
it's poised on the drive next door
ready for anything,
snub-nosed, eyes shining.

Behind it the house is growing,
diggers churning out noise.
First a summerhouse then a pool,
something they call a pergola.

Only the car bothers me,
it sits there, purring by the kerb.
Inches away you scarcely hear it.
It never roars.

He stopped me on Monday
babbled about acceleration,
power steering, optimum speed.
He stays out in it until late.

Sometimes his wife looks lonely.
I wait in my garden
to catch sight of her upstairs.
Normally she only waves.

But today she leant down to me,
blonde hair spilling across the ledge,
her bodywork perfect
under her blouse.

CLOUDY CONDITIONS

From the window I can see Geography,
blinds half-down for an afternoon
of stratus and nimbus, mackerel skies.

Blustered all day between classroom
and staff room, I realise now
the resignation on my desk must be given in.

I'm ashamed of it, like homework badly done.
The weather has stopped temporarily,
my class must be struggling to understand

thunderheads, pileus, rain.
In my hand the envelope is light and see-through,
ready to begin its climb.

Maybe it will carry me with it –
a trail of cirrus, flimsy,
a little too thin for a silver lining.

MOTHING

Painting sweetness
onto sweetness,
I bless the cane
with my catcher's mix.

Lepidoptera.
Night drops them
through the sticky dusk
in paper handfuls.

They stir past my face
unsettle the air,
wings snagging
against the dark.

The whole family comes to me:
emerald, codling, silk,
antennae weighted
with last night's theft.

I bring them home
through corridors of light,
start their sweet drowning
their brittle panic.

Each morning
I clean the knotted stems,
dismantle the mosaic
of broken wings.

INSTANTANEOUS

Until the phone rings
you've been stored away,
three polaroids bleached almost to nothing
safe in a shoebox under my bed.

The news of your death sounds invented –
last train home to Brighton, drunk
head out of the window to catch the air,
smiling while the dark rushed at you.

There was no time to scream.
Your wife fainted in the corridor,
dreamed of ways to reassemble you.
By now the phone's fallen

back on its hook. But it's too late.
Images of you arrive by the carriage load,
flicker past me like a train
that is not scheduled to stop.

STORAGE

He keeps the past under his bed,
childhood summers archived
in cardboard boxes.

At night they leak sunshine,
voices calling from the swimming hole.
His marriage is folded away
in a suitcase with a broken lock.

When he opens it, he finds it empty.
His wife left only the smells
of their honeymoon –
citrus groves, red wine, skin.

The present is more confusing.
Days of the week, mealtimes,
visitors' names are all forgotten,
but the boxes are a comfort.

Huddled shoulder to shoulder,
close knit as armour plate
they keep noise out, warmth in.

PARADISE ROAD

It starts well
the Majestic cinema on the corner,
lilies twisting heavenwards
through every window.

Further on the antique shop's full.
Dressers heavy with pottery,
gangs of toby jugs
edging towards the door.

In the café, an old woman
keeps a laundry bag for company.
It slumps in the chair opposite
while she finishes her cake.

The jeweller and pawnbroker
are promising the world,
loans for anyone on anything
from a wristwatch to a car.

All that's left is St Peters,
gates padlocked, day-glow graffiti
splattered across the wall.
But there's no need to give up.

Sitting on a gravestone
a couple learn how to kiss,
fumbling each others' faces
with their mouths.